Take Care of Yourself

Resting

Siân Smith

www.raintreepublishers.co.uk
Visit our website to find out
more information about
Raintree books.

To order:

☎ Phone 0845 6044371
🖷 Fax +44 (0) 1865 312263
🖳 Email myorders@raintreepublishers.co.uk

Customers from outside the UK please telephone +44 1865 312262

Raintree is an imprint of Capstone Global Library Limited,
a company incorporated in England and Wales having
its registered office at 7 Pilgrim Street, London, EC4V 6LB–
Registered company number: 6695582

Edited by Dan Nunn, Rebecca Rissman,
    and John-Paul Wilkins
Designed by Victoria Allen
Picture research by Tracy Cummins
Production by Alison Parsons
Originated by Capstone Global Library Ltd
Printed and bound in China by Leo Paper Products Ltd

ISBN 978 1 406 24163 1
16 15 14 13 12
10 9 8 7 6 5 4 3 2 1

British Library Cataloguing in Publication Data
Smith, Siân.
Resting. – (Take care of yourself)
613.7'9-dc22
A full catalogue record for this book is available from the
British Library.

Acknowledgements
We would like to thank the following for permission to
reproduce photographs: Corbis pp. 10 (© moodboard),
15 (© Heide Benser), 23a (© Christina Kennedy/DK
Stock); Getty Images pp. 7 (Martin Barraud), 8 (B. Blue),
11 (ColorBlind), 17 (Comstock), 18 (Siri Stafford), 20
(Jupiterimages); istockphoto pp. 5 (© Ana Abejon), 6
(© Troels Graugaard), 12 (© Nikolay Titov), 16 (© Amanda
Rohde), 19 (© darren wise), 21 (© Robert Churchill);
Shutterstock pp. 4, 23c (© StockLite), 9 (© Monkey Business
Images), 13, 22 (© AISPIX), 14, 23b (© wavebreakmedia ltd).

Front cover photograph of girl (4-6) sleeping in grass,
elevated view reproduced with permission of Getty Images
(Mike Harrington). Rear cover photograph of sleeping child
reproduced with permission of istockphoto (© Ana Abejon).

Every effort has been made to contact copyright holders
of material reproduced in this book. Any omissions will be
rectified in subsequent printings if notice is given to the
publisher.

We would like to thank Nancy Harris and Dee Reid for their
assistance in the preparation of this book.

Contents

Rest

When you rest you take time to relax and not do very much.

The best rest you can get is sleep.

How does sleep help my body?

Your body needs sleep to stay healthy.

Sleep gives your body time
to fix itself.

Sleep gives your body time to turn food into things you need.

Sleep gives your brain time to sort out things you have learnt.

Sleep gives your body time
to grow.

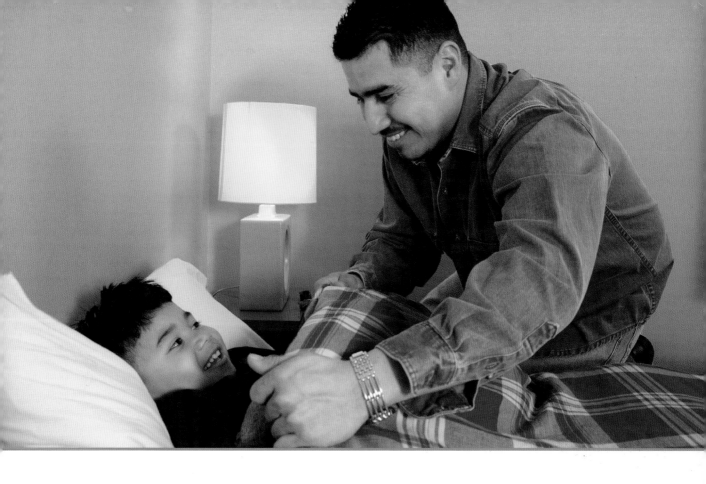

When you are young you need
to sleep more.

How can I help my body rest?

Give your body some time to rest every day.

Do some exercise every day.
This will help you to sleep at night.

Eat lots of healthy foods every day.

Have a shower or bath in
the evening.

Do something peaceful before you go to bed.

You could listen to a story or some music.

Go to bed at bedtime.

You need to go to bed at bedtime, even if you do not feel tired.

If you cannot sleep, just lie down
and close your eyes.

This will help your body to get ready for the next day.

Can you remember?

What can you do in the day to help you sleep at night?

22

Answer on page 24

Picture glossary

 **exercise** moving your body around to keep healthy

 **peaceful** calm, quiet, and relaxing

 **rest** take time to relax and not do very much

Index

Answer to question on page 22
You can do some exercise in the day to help you sleep at night.

Notes for parents and teachers
Before reading
Ask the children what rest is. When we rest we take time to relax and give our bodies a chance to recover from the things we have been doing. The best kind of rest we can get is sleep. We need to sleep to keep our bodies healthy. Do the children think that children need more, less, or the same amount of sleep as adults? Read the book together to find out.

After reading
Make a list with the children of all the ways in which sleep helps our bodies. Help the children to make a "Why I need sleep" wheel from two card circles joined with a split pin. Use a pencil and ruler to divide the bottom circle into four equal quarters. Children can record and illustrate one of the reasons they need sleep in each section. Cut a quarter out of the second circle. Place this on top and join the two circles with the split pin, so that each section can be revealed as the wheel is turned.